An Executive Perspective on Workforce Planning

Robert M. Emmerichs

Cheryl Y. Marcum

Albert A. Robbert

T0162205

Prepared for the Office of the Secretary of Defense

RAND
National Defense Research Institute

The research described in this report was sponsored by the Office of the Secretary of Defense (OSD). The research was conducted in the RAND National Defense Research Institute, a federally funded research and development center supported by the OSD, the Joint Staff, the unified commands, and the defense agencies under Contract DASW01-01-C-0004.

Library of Congress Cataloging-in-Publication Data

Emmerichs, Robert M.
    An executive perspective on workforce planning / Robert M. Emmerichs,
Cheryl Y. Marcum, Albert A. Robbert.
      p. cm.
    "MR-1684/2."
    Includes bibliographical references.
    ISBN 0-8330-3453-7 (pbk.)
      1. United States—Armed Forces—Procurement. 2. United States—Armed
Forces—Personnel management. 3. Manpower planning—United States. I.
Marcum, Cheryl Y. II. Robbert, Albert A., 1944– III. Rand Corporation. IV.Title.

    UC263.E278 2003
    355.6'1'0973—dc22

                  2003016511

The RAND Corporation is a nonprofit research organization providing objective analysis and effective solutions that address the challenges facing the public and private sectors around the world. RAND's publications do not necessarily reflect the opinions of its research clients and sponsors.

RAND® is a registered trademark.

Cover design by Barbara Angell Caslon

Published 2004 by RAND
1700 Main Street, P.O. Box 2138, Santa Monica, CA 90407-2138
1200 South Hayes Street, Arlington, VA 22202-5050
201 North Craig Street, Suite 202, Pittsburgh, PA 15213-1516
RAND URL: http://www.rand.org/
To order RAND documents or to obtain additional information, contact
Distribution Services: Telephone: (310) 451-7002;
Fax: (310) 451-6915; Email: order@rand.org

The Acquisition 2005 Task Force final report, *Shaping the Civilian Acquisition Workforce of the Future* (Office of the Secretary of Defense, 2000), called for the development and implementation of needs-based human resource performance plans for Department of Defense (DoD) civilian acquisition workforces. This need was premised on unusually heavy workforce turnover and an expected transformation in acquisition products and methods during the early part of the 21st century. The Director of Acquisition Education, Training and Career Development within the Office of the Deputy Under Secretary of Defense for Acquisition Reform, in collaboration with the Deputy Assistant Secretary of Defense for Civilian Personnel Policy, asked the RAND Corporation to assist the Office of the Secretary of Defense (OSD) and several of the defense components in formulating the first iteration of these plans and then evaluating the components' plans.

As part of this project, RAND identified, and described in this document, the critical role that corporate and line executives play in the workforce planning activity. A companion report, *An Operational Process for Workforce Planning*, MR-1684/1-OSD, completes the context for this work and describes a methodology any organization can use to conduct workforce planning.

This report will be of interest to executives in the DoD acquisition and human resource management communities as the workforce planning activity continues to mature. In addition, it is oriented and will be more generally of interest to other executives—both within and outside the DoD—whose organizations and functions face a similar need for workforce planning.

This research was conducted for the Under Secretary of Defense for Acquisition, Technology, and Logistics and the Under Secretary of Defense for Personnel and Readiness within the Forces and Resources Policy Center of RAND National Defense Research Institute, a federally funded research and development center sponsored by the Office of the Secretary of Defense, the Joint Staff, the unified commands, and the defense agencies.

Comments are welcome and may be addressed to the project leader, Albert A. Robbert at Al_Robbert@rand.org, 703-413-1100, Ext. 5308.

For more information on the Forces and Resources Policy Center, contact the director, Susan Everingham, susan_everingham@ rand.org, 310-393-0411, Ext. 7654. RAND Corporation, 1700 Main Street, Santa Monica, California 90401-2138.

CONTENTS

FIGURES

TABLES

SUMMARY

Workforce planning is an organizational activity intended to ensure that investment in human capital results in the timely capability to effectively carry out the organization's strategic intent.[1] Specifically, the activity seeks

- to obtain a clear representation of the workforce needed to accomplish the organization's strategic intent

- to develop an aligned set of human resource management policies and practices[2]—in other words, a comprehensive plan of action—that will ensure the appropriate workforce will be available when needed

- to establish a convincing rationale—a business case—for acquiring new authority and marshalling resources to implement the human resource management policies and programs needed to accomplish the organization's strategic intent.

---

[1]We define *strategic intent* as an expression (sometimes explicit, but often implicit) of what business the organization is in (or wants to be in) and how the organization's leaders plan to carry out that business. Leaders usually express strategic intent in the organization's strategic planning documents. In particular, the business the organization is in (or wants to be in) is often outlined in a vision, mission, and/or purpose statement. How the leaders choose to carry out the business is often captured in goals, guiding principles, and/or strategies. A major task for workforce planners is to identify explicitly those elements of strategic intent that workforce characteristics help accomplish.

[2]*Human resource management policies and practices* are the tools managers use to shape the workforce. An *aligned set of policies and practices* supports the leaders' strategic intent (i.e., the policies and practices are vertically aligned) and are mutually reinforcing (i.e., they are horizontally aligned).

RAND developed an approach any organization can use to conduct workforce planning.[3] This approach focuses on answering four central questions:

1. What critical workforce characteristics will the organization need in the future to accomplish its strategic intent, and what is the desired distribution of these characteristics?

2. What is the distribution—in today's workforce—of the workforce characteristics needed for the future?

3. If the organization maintains current policies and programs, what distribution of characteristics will the future workforce possess?

4. What changes to human resource management policies and practices, resource decisions, and other actions will eliminate or alleviate gaps (overages or shortages) between the future desired distribution and the projected future inventory?

An organization may become aware of workforce planning and initially engage in it to respond to an emerging crisis—for example, to ameliorate the impact of potentially large numbers of retirements in the next decade. This application of workforce planning, however, may not benefit enough from the unique contributions of executives to overcome the cost of their involvement. But if an organization engages in a more strategic application—shaping the workforce to achieve changing organizational ends—not only do executive contributions benefit workforce planning, they are essential to it.

Executives contribute to strategic workforce planning by providing guidance focused on what results the organization should produce and determining how the organization will produce those results. The first is primarily a role for the most-senior executives of the organization's corporate headquarters; the second, primarily a role for the executives and line managers in a business unit, together with its community and human resource managers.

---

[3]RAND developed this approach for the DoD acquisition community. Six DoD components completed an initial cycle of workforce planning for its acquisition community using this approach in the summer of 2001. This report builds on their experience to refine and to generalize the executive perspective.

This report presents an executive perspective of workforce planning. It concentrates on the means by which executives guide the process—both *what* they do and *how* they do it. We focus on large organizations with many levels of hierarchy, for example, the DoD or most other federal agencies. Such organizations possess a common purpose and mission, accomplished through the coordinated efforts of heterogeneous divisions, functions, and business units. Consequently, several executive perspectives (corporate, functional, business unit, for example) bear on workforce planning.

We recommend that large organizations fully involve their business units in conducting workforce planning as well as in conducting other major activities of human capital strategic planning. The human capital implications are best defined at the business unit level. The business unit is responsible for employing that human capital, and the business unit decides *how* it is going to employ it.

The business units, of course, are part of the larger organization, serving the larger organization's overall mission. The corporate headquarters is responsible for setting the stage—providing the fundamental description of what results the functional communities and the business units should produce to support the larger organization as a whole. If a change in internal direction is not envisioned, the role of the business units in accomplishing the larger organization's overall mission may already be well understood and embedded in the fabric of daily operation. In such a case, the business units might employ workforce planning as an autonomous activity. However, if senior corporate executives seek to implement a change in the organization's overall operating and/or functional strategy, they must clearly articulate their intent—the corporate and/or functional strategic intent—and communicate it to the business units to shape *what* activities the business units carry out and *how* they do it.

How can corporate executives provide this guidance from the top of the organization to the business units that actually carry out the diverse activities necessary to successfully accomplish the organization's strategy? We propose the framework in Figure S.1 as a context for ensuring that the strategic intent of the organization's corporate executives influences in a meaningful way what the business units do and how they carry out their activities. (We use the acquisition function as a representation of one of the several functional perspectives within an organization.)

In this context, a major change in strategy (or significant change in the environment) usually implies a major change in the capabilities required to carry out the strategy. Often, the most important of these capabilities are embedded in the organization's human capital. When that is the case, workforce planning is one of the primary means senior leaders can use to execute the desired shift in direction. Workforce planning can align the capabilities inherent in human capital with the new way of doing business.

Workforce planning takes place within the framework of human capital strategic planning. Human capital strategic planning provides

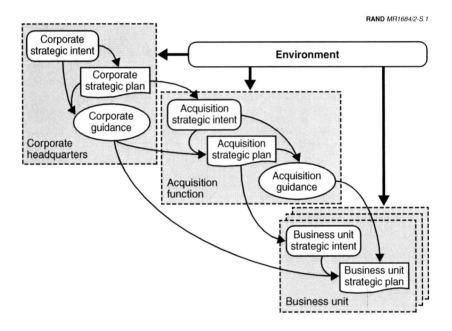

Figure S.1—Relationships Among Strategic Intent, Guidance, and Plan
from Multiple Organizational Perspectives

the means with which to align the full range of human capital decisions with organizational ends.

Comprehensive human capital strategic planning comprises at least four separate processes: cultural shaping, organizational design, workforce planning, and performance planning. These processes focus on organizational values, organizational characteristics (authority, communication, etc.), workforce characteristics, and behaviors, respectively. Figure S.2 portrays the context for these processes from the business unit's perspective. The strategic intent articulated in corporate and functional guidance,[4] together with a

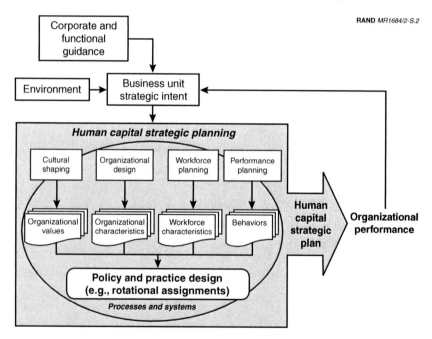

Figure S.2—A Framework for Human Capital Strategic Planning

---

[4]*Corporate* and *functional* guidance (as we employ the terms in this report) transmit the aspects of corporate and functional strategic intent that influence human capital strategic planning at the business unit level.

business unit's own strategic intent and its environment,[5] is the starting point for each of the activities.

In the context of human capital strategic planning, senior leaders—corporate executives, executives and line leaders in business units, together with community[6] and human resource managers—can use workforce planning to shape the capabilities of their workforces and thereby influence how the business units carry out their missions.

Table S.1 summarizes the major workforce planning roles of senior leaders throughout an organization.

We recommend that executives take seven actions to influence and improve workforce planning.

1. Institute workforce planning as an integral part of organizational strategic planning

2. Provide clear guidance

3. Ensure the right participants

4. Lead the effort—physically and intellectually

5. Focus on the business case

6. Monitor results

7. Act on any viable business case produced.

---

[5]We define the *environment* as external factors that impact the organization but over which the organization has little or no control.

[6]Many organizations assign career development and other human resource–related responsibilities for individuals in specific occupational or professional groups to senior executives in the occupation or professional group. In addition, senior executives often oversee these types of responsibilities for individuals working in major functional areas (such as acquisition or finance). These *community managers* (or *functional community managers*) are expected to ensure that the workforce possesses the capabilities needed by business units.

Table S.1

Executive Roles in Workforce Planning

	Formulate Strategic Intent	Organize for Workforce Planning	Interest and Motivate Workforce Planning Participants
Senior corporate executives	Formulate corporate and functional guidance with implications for human capital	Assign appropriate workforce planning roles throughout the organization	Generate the need; identify the benefit; act on results; take on difficult changes
Business unit executives and line managers	Articulate business unit strategic intent in terms of its human capital implications	Integrate workforce planning into organizational strategic planning	Actively participate; act on the results
Functional community managers	Specify a vision and a community management strategy for the functional community	Align community management structure to respond to business needs	Promote partnership between line managers and community managers
Human resource managers	Formulate an organization-centric human resource management strategy	Sponsor workforce planning; develop center of excellence	Develop innovative human capital solutions to problems identified during workforce planning

ACKNOWLEDGMENTS

The research underlying this report had its genesis in the Office of the Deputy Assistant Secretary of Defense for Civilian Personnel Policy and the Office of Acquisition Education, Training and Career Development in the Office of the Assistant Secretary of Defense for Acquisition Reform. They recognized the need for better workforce planning capabilities, particularly with respect to Defense acquisition workforces, and they committed resources to providing those capabilities, including sponsorship of our research and assistance. We received valuable advice and assistance from many individuals within these offices.

Part of our research took us into close contact with two acquisition business units—the Space and Naval Warfare Systems Command (SPAWAR) and the Naval Facilities Engineering Command (NAVFAC). The leadership of Rear Admiral Kenneth Slaght (SPAWAR) and Rear Admiral Michael Loose (NAVFAC) was one of the most valuable contributions to our research. A number of individuals in those commands helped us make our consultations productive, including Margaret Malowney, Director of Human Resources at SPAWAR; Margaret Craig, Executive and Defense Acquisition Workforce Improvement Act Training Coordinator at SPAWAR; Amy Younts, Director of Community Management at NAVFAC; Sara Buescher, Director of Civilian Personnel Program, NAVFAC; Joy Bird, Associate Director of Community Management, NAVFAC; and Hal Kohn, Senior Systems Analyst for Community Management, NAVFAC.

This effort builds on the conceptual foundation of strategic human resource management propounded by the presidentially chartered

Eighth Quadrennial Review of Military Compensation in 1997, which was further refined and applied by the Naval Personnel Task Force, which was convened by the Secretary of the Navy and the Assistant Secretary of the Navy for Manpower and Reserve Affairs in 1999.

RAND colleague Harry Thie and Steve Kelman, Professor of Public Management at the Kennedy School of Government, Harvard University, provided thoughtful reviews of the work. Miriam Polon edited the manuscript. Any remaining errors are, of course, our own.

DAWIA	Defense Acquisition Workforce Improvement Act
DoD	Department of Defense
GAO	U.S. General Accounting Office
NAVFAC	Naval Facilities Engineering Command
OSD	Office of the Secretary of Defense
SPAWAR	Space and Naval Warfare Systems Command

Chapter One

INTRODUCTION

Workforce planning can be a critical strategic activity, enabling an organization to identify, develop, and sustain the workforce capabilities it needs to successfully accomplish its mission in a dynamically changing environment. This activity can lead to decisions that establish the fundamental composition of the workforce and the means to achieve that composition. Because these decisions can directly influence the organization's ability to conduct day-to-day operations and—even more fundamentally—its ability to accomplish long-term goals, workforce planning can be an important executive responsibility for senior leaders.

From an operational perspective, the effects of insufficient workforce planning often manifest themselves slowly. Initially, managers might experience the effect on daily operations as an irritant. For example, the time to fill vacancies, particularly for experienced journeymen, lengthens. Only as a crisis looms (say, as vacancies affect the organization's ability to meet important commitments) might managers identify increasing competition for talent and growing internal demands for that talent as the major causes. At this stage, however, managers may have few options, short of a bidding war, with which to respond, driving up costs and potentially reducing near-term organizational performance.

To envision the possible impact of inadequate workforce planning more dramatically, consider the consequences of the "hemorrhage of talent" from the military during the mid-1970s: At that time, ships were held in port and Army leaders warned of a "hollow force." Now, DoD officials are expressing similar alarm as the implications of the impending retirement of a significant proportion of the federal civil service workforces during the next decade are becoming better understood—especially the difficulty of replacing such a large number of experienced employees in a short time in a tight labor market. Although the impending crisis differs in nature and cause from the crisis of the mid-1970s, the upcoming retirements in the federal workforce have led the General Accounting Office (GAO) to declare human capital at risk (GAO, 2001, p. 71 ff.) and led the Office of Management and Budget and the Office of Personnel Management (Ballard, 2001) to express serious concerns over the consequences. Undoubtedly, senior leaders will be held accountable for the significant operational implications of this situation.

Workforce planning can help senior leaders avoid or ameliorate such problems. More important, however, it can provide them a means of aligning the capabilities of the workforce with the direction the leaders want the organization to go. Senator George V. Voinovich, chairman of the Subcommittee on Oversight of Governmental Management, Restructuring and the District of Columbia, recommended that "the president should direct all federal departments and agencies to conduct comprehensive workforce planning as part of the Results Act strategic planning activities, to determine attrition, hiring, skills requirements for the next decade, and the kind of workforce that will be needed in the next 15–20 years" (2000, p. 47). In other words, when they take a strategic perspective, an organization's senior leaders can use workforce planning as a powerful tool for accomplishing their strategic goals.

Managers wield a vast armamentarium of human resource management policies and practices with which to motivate and shape the workforce. However, whether countering operational problems, enhancing organizational performance, or reshaping the workforce to ensure the ability to achieve long-term goals, successful solutions generally take time. Workforce planning identifies actions (changes in human resource management policies and practices) leaders can take at the *present time* to implement fundamental organizational change and to avoid or ameliorate problems likely to arise in the *future*.

This report views workforce planning as a strategic tool in which senior leaders play a critical role—both in championing the workforce planning activity and in participating in it. In fact, active participation is a key success factor. Accordingly, we target this report to senior leaders.[1]

We begin, in Chapter Two, with a description of the need for workforce planning from an executive perspective and the strategic purpose toward which the activity is directed. In Chapter Three, we show that organizational strategic planning is a major executive responsibility because it is the means by which senior leaders convert their long-term goals into actions. Workforce planning is only one such means within organizational strategic planning in general and human capital strategic planning in particular. However, organizational strategic planning is the unique source of information—in the form of strategic intent[2]—essential to effective human capital strategic planning and workforce planning. Consequently, we describe the larger strategic context, focusing on the role of senior leaders in developing strategic intent and guidance to influence the product of workforce planning. We then position the workforce planning activity within the context of human capital strategic planning. In Chapter Four, which focuses on basic executive functions, we describe the participants in the workforce planning activity and their roles. We conclude, in Chapter Five, by recommending specific actions that leaders can take to enhance the effectiveness of the workforce planning activity.

---

[1]We generally mean to include the following in the term *senior leaders*: at the corporate level, the organization's most-senior executives, both those in operational positions and those heading staff functions (such as acquisition or human resource management); at the business level, its business unit executives, line managers, community managers, and functional managers.

[2]We define *strategic intent* as an expression (sometimes explicit, but often implicit) of what business the organization is in (or wants to be in) and how the organization's leaders plan to carry out that business. Leaders usually express strategic intent in the organization's strategic planning documents. In particular, the business the organization is in (or wants to be in) is often outlined in a vision, mission, and/or purpose statement. How the leaders choose to carry out the business is often captured in goals, guiding principles, and/or strategies. A major task for workforce planners is to identify explicitly those elements of strategic intent that workforce characteristics help accomplish.

Chapter Two

NEEDS AND PURPOSES

Workforce planning is an activity that supports leaders' decisions about the workforce. It is, however, an expensive activity. Executed properly, workforce planning requires a substantial amount of senior leaders' time, an extensive array of information, and sophisticated analytic capabilities (for example, econometric and inventory projection models). An organization should expend these resources only if the action will favorably affect the quality of workforce decisions and, ultimately, the outcomes that are important to the organization. In this chapter, we outline why we believe many organizations face workforce planning needs that justify these resource expenditures. We then outline the purposes of workforce planning in terms that respond to these needs.

NEEDS FOR WORKFORCE PLANNING

Workforce planning is not always a strategic activity that requires executive participation. For example, an organization operating in a relatively stable environment can accomplish its mission effectively without engaging in workforce planning and incurring the associated expenses. Its future workforce will be largely the same as its current workforce. The decisions to acquire, develop, and refresh the workforce will have evolved over time, will be well-understood and implemented, and will ensure that the workforce needed in the future is available.

For most organizations, however, the environment has not been stable, and it may change even more substantially and rapidly in the future.[1] In addition, because of the fluctuating environment, the composition of today's workforce is a direct result of past decisions linked to unique circumstances, not a result of a stable, well-understood set of decisions applicable in the future—even if that future were stable.[2] And because the environment is likely to continue to change in the future, the future workforce will differ, in some cases substantially, from today's workforce, requiring different decisions from those previously executed.[3]

Finally, the business model is changing in many organizations. Whether because of increased reliance on "best practices" or as a result of the "revolution in business affairs," the composition of the workforce needed for a change in direction will differ from that of the present.

Senior leaders are best-positioned to understand and interpret the external pressures and, especially, to articulate the direction in which the organization needs to move to accomplish its vision of how it wants to do business in the future. Workforce planning translates these executive inputs into decisions that ensure that the requisite human capital is available to the organization when needed.

External Pressures

External pressures affect the needed workforce composition and the organization's ability to acquire and sustain it. Although it is not

---

[1] For example, the DoD reduced its civilian workforce by approximately 30 percent during the 1990s in response to changes in the global political-military situation. The labor market, particularly for high-quality talent, has become more competitive, and trends in the economy have created shortages in critical skills (for example, information technology specialists).

[2] For example, the reduction in the DoD civilian workforce was largely accomplished by reducing the number of new hires, resulting today in a smaller pool than historically available from which to develop experienced workers to replace the expected higher-than-normal loss of senior (and experienced) workers due to retirement.

[3] For example, the evolving implications of the new security environment, of e-government, and of the post-dot-com economy have yet to work themselves out, but as they become clear, the implications will potentially affect the work—and the workforce—of many organizations inside and outside the federal government.

within the scope of this report to fully elaborate on these pressures, from the perspective of many federal agencies, three pressures are representative: shifting views of work, competition in the labor market, and the rate of change of technology.

Shifting Views of Work. Federal human resource management systems rely, to varying degrees, on the assumption that people are largely motivated to pursue careers that are managed by and tightly coupled to a single lifelong employer. This assumption proved generally valid in the past.[4] In fact, the current situation—in which a majority of civilian employees are nearing retirement eligibility—is, in part, the result of individuals wanting to stay with the organization to achieve the security of the retirement system, and of organizational decisions (reflected in human resource management policies and practices) that enabled and even motivated that desire. Today and in the future, however, this assumption may provide a weak foundation upon which to build human resource management policies and practices.

An observable shift is under way from the traditional and familiar organization-managed career to the individual-managed career. The concept of the individual-managed career recognizes that individual choices result in accumulation of a comprehensive set of diverse life experiences including education, training, a variety of jobs—even changes in occupational fields—in a variety of organizations, and volunteer work. Hall labeled the individual-managed career (which the individual shapes more than the organization shapes) the "protean career."[5] He observed that one of the defining characteristics of the individual-managed career is the individual's ability to redirect it from time to time to meet the individual's personal needs. (Hall, 1996, p. 20 [citing Hall, 1976, p. 201]). Many members of the generation entering the workforce today appear to view work and their relationship with an employer differently from

---

[4]In 1986 (the most recent year surveyed), a survey published in the *Occupational Outlook Quarterly*, summer 1989, reported that about 10 percent of all U.S. workers actually changed careers (Bolles, 2002). Six years later, in 1992, a survey by the Roper Organization for Shearson Lehman Brothers found that 45 percent of all U.S. workers said they would change careers if they could (Bolles, 2002).

[5]"Protean" comes from the Greek god Proteus, who had the ability to change shape at will—for example, "from wild boar to fire to tree" (Hall, 1996).

members of previous generations. For example, such characteristics as fierce independence, high correlation of retention with continued training and learning, increased importance of work/life balance, and disdain for bureaucracy,[6] if manifest in large portions of the workforce, could have a significant effect on the supply of qualified new hires and on the turnover rate of current employees. Human resource management policies and practices that sustained the workforce in the past may not be effective in the future. Workforce planning provides a set of analytic tools with which to investigate these potential problems and to identify timely solutions.

Labor-Market Competition. Competition for qualified employees has risen to the level of a "war for talent." Not only are managers finding it more difficult than in the past to recruit the talent needed, they are experiencing greater difficulty retaining that talent. Policies and practices that worked previously may be less effective in this changed environment. Workforce planning provides a structured framework within which to investigate comprehensive strategies for winning the war for talent.

Technology Change. The rate of technology change may also affect the composition of the workforce needed in the future. In some areas, for example, current knowledge may become more important than experience. Today, career paths reflect a structure that supports the accretion of experience over generally long periods. That structure may not be supportable in the future. Workforce planning provides the information upon which to design and evaluate alternative career management strategies.

Internal Opportunities

Internal decisions (ranging from execution of past practices to reformulation of the business strategy) also affect the needed workforce composition and the organization's ability to acquire and sustain that composition. Consider three specific examples from the DoD.

---

[6]Characteristics of "Gen-Xers" reported in Zemke, Filipczak, and Raines, 1999.

A Large Retirement-Eligible Workforce. The Acquisition Workforce 2005 Task Force expressed major concern regarding the potentially heavy turnover of retirement-eligible employees in the coming decade. Its report observes that this eventuality demands the immediate implementation of comprehensive workforce planning. Recognizing that the composition of the current workforce arose, in large part, from implementation of a patchwork of generally unrelated policies designed to resolve ad hoc problems, the report suggests that workforce planning (in conjunction with the departure of large numbers from the workforce) provides an opportunity to purposefully align the workforce to achieve clearly articulated objectives.

Increased Reliance on Contractors. Traditionally, DoD organizations have made decisions affecting the military workforce independent of decisions affecting the civilian workforce, and both in turn, have made decisions independent of the contractor workforce—in particular, those contractors providing direct support within the organization. For example, outsourcing work that is not inherently governmental means fewer military and civilian positions through which to advance and perhaps fewer "interesting" positions to fill. The people filling the inherently governmental positions that remain (for example, those providing direction and oversight to the contractor force) will require sufficient technical knowledge to manage the contractor force—knowledge that can, in part, often be developed only experientially. Although these considerations should not be a primary factor upon which to base outsourcing decisions, they should inform and shape decisions concerning the organization, management, and reward of the remaining federal workforce. Workforce planning can be the mechanism for integrating and aligning decisions affecting all three workforces.

New Acquisition Strategies. The report of the second Quadrennial Defense Review (Department of Defense, 2001, pp. 40, 41) describes a shift in direction that may affect how the DoD acquires its weapon systems. This shift in strategic direction is characterized by a capabilities-based approach; research and development to ensure a decisive lead in transformation-critical technologies; a focus on key transformational initiatives and selective recapitalization of the legacy force; and increasing reliance on the private sector for much of the leadership in developing new technologies. As this corporate strategic intent crystallizes, it is likely to influence how an acquisition business unit carries out its mission. In particular, a new strategic direction may well require people with different characteristics from those of the acquisition workforce today—as well as more of some existing characteristics and less of others. Without the appropriate workforce composition, the revised acquisition strategy is unlikely to be fully effective. And while significant shifts in the needed workforce characteristics may take years to achieve, the shift will not effectively begin until the target characteristics are identified.

Unlike external pressures or past decisions (where the major product of workforce planning is to identify and respond to forces outside the organization's control), implementing the leaders' strategic direction relies on workforce planning as a critical lever for organizational change. It becomes a powerful executive resource to transform how the organization does business.

PURPOSES OF STRATEGIC WORKFORCE PLANNING

In the context of these external pressures and internal opportunities, an organization may employ workforce planning to accomplish at least three purposes:

- to obtain a clear representation of the workforce needed to accomplish the organization's strategic intent

- to develop an aligned set of human-resource management policies and practices[7]—in other words, a comprehensive plan of action—that will ensure the appropriate workforce will be available when needed

- to establish a convincing rationale—a business case—for acquiring new authority and marshalling resources to implement the human resource management policies and programs needed to accomplish the organization's strategic intent.

An organization can conduct workforce planning without explicit reference to strategic intent. For example, a stable organization op-

---

[7]Human resource management policies and practices are the tools managers use to shape the workforce. An aligned set of policies and practices supports the leaders' strategic intent (i.e., the policies and practices are vertically aligned) and are mutually reinforcing (i.e., they are horizontally aligned).

erating in a stable environment, where future workforce needs mirror current needs, can employ simple workforce planning to identify its hiring, training, and promotion needs over the programming and budgeting horizon. We call this activity *tactical* workforce planning. In this context, the purpose of workforce planning is to support requests for training and development resources and to enable succession planning; it does not require active executive participation. In other words, an organization can conduct tactical workforce planning largely as a "staff drill."

Generally, however, this is not the environment in which most federal agencies find themselves. The future *is* likely to be different—in terms of what external factors impinge on the organization or, more importantly, how the organization wants to do business. In this case, *strategic* workforce planning, driven by strategic intent, can pay large dividends.[8] Strategic workforce planning, therefore, requires leaders to articulate their strategic intent. Without a clear articulation of strategic intent, workforce planning is likely to devolve into its tactical form, resulting in marginal changes to the composition of the workforce. The outcome is likely to be similar if senior leaders view workforce planning primarily as a staff exercise. Senior leaders must actively participate—physically and intellectually—to realize the results they intend. This report is about *strategic* workforce planning.

---

[8]Importantly, these dividends can be quantified (in monetary and organizational performance terms). For a brief summary of the kinds of quantifiable impacts that changes to human resource management policies and practices have had on organizations, see "Working Paper on Quantifying the Benefits of Changing the Way Organizations Reward, Organize and Manage People" (Department of Defense, 1997). For instance, one of the examples (directly related to policies and practices that might be used to improve retention to meet workforce needs) cited in the working paper focused on the evaluation of broadbanding (a pay policy linked to performance) in federal government demonstration projects: "Reduced turnover of high performers. Turnover among high performers was reduced by 50 percent in the Navy demonstration labs. Between 1984 and 1992 turnover of top-rated scientists averaged 3.5 percent compared to 5.5 percent at the comparison sites," and "Increased turnover of low performers. During a 10-year period, turnover of marginal and unacceptable performers ranged from 20 to 50 percent. Those who were not separated improved their performance." The literature has recently shown a renewed emphasis on developing methodologies to capture and articulate the value that human resource management policies and practices contribute to an organization (see, for example, Fitz-enz, 1990; 1995; 2000; and Phillips, Stone, and Phillips, 2001).

Chapter Three

CONTEXT: ORGANIZATIONAL AND HUMAN CAPITAL STRATEGIC PLANNING

Organizational strategic planning provides the context for human capital strategic planning. Human capital strategic planning provides the context for workforce planning. Each form of planning is an executive responsibility. This chapter briefly describes these three contexts.

ORGANIZATIONAL STRATEGIC PLANNING: FOCUSING ON STRATEGIC INTENT

Strategic planning in general—and human capital strategic planning in particular—is complicated by the size and scope of a large organization with diverse missions. At the least, such an organization exhibits corporate, functional, and business unit perspectives.[1] In addition, the focus and content of strategic planning differ among perspectives.[2] The interaction among the different perspectives on strategy in an organization has been investigated by a number of authors (for a particularly comprehensive example see Hax and

---

[1] In addition, the organization may be structured to include several corporate levels; in the DeoD for example, the Office of the Secretary of Defense (OSD) and the military department headquarters might both be considered corporate level. Similarly, a functional perspective may exist at several levels.

[2] Strategic planning may also include other dimensions such as information technology, financial management, physical plant, and human resources. We limit our discussion to the human resource dimension, but most of the discussion applies to other dimensions as well.

Majluf, 1996). We build on that foundation and discuss each perspective in turn.

The Corporate Headquarters Perspective

From the corporate perspective, planning focuses on the fundamental mission of the organization and, in the broadest terms, on what each component part of the organization will do to help accomplish that mission. In DoD, for example, documents such as *Joint Vision 2020* and the *Quadrennial Defense Review* convey the corporate strategic intent. Documents such as the *National Military Strategy* (at the DoD level) and *The Army Plan* (at the military department level) translate the corporate strategic intent into the means required to accomplish the desired ends. Such documents contain implications for strategic planning within the functional communities and at the business units. Unfortunately, these implications are typically implicit in the reference documents rather than explicit.

Analyzing these documents and explicitly summarizing key corporate guidance will ensure clear and uniform direction to the strategic planning activity within the functions and business units. This guidance will differ depending on the focus of the strategic planning effort. In the case of human capital strategic planning, effective guidance highlights the human resource implications of the corporate strategic intent and the strategic plan.[3] Thus, corporate guidance (as we employ the term in this report) is the vehicle for identifying and transmitting those aspects of corporate strategic intent that directly affect human capital strategic planning.

Ideally, the overarching documents clearly state this guidance. Unfortunately—particularly in the case of human capital—the implications are usually ambiguous or obscure. Clarifying the human resource implications of strategic intent ensures that subsequent

---

[3]For example, in preparation for an initial application of workforce planning in the defense acquisition community, the OSD ncluded guidance to "reduce the reliance on military personnel in the acquisition community." This statement reflected a corporate decision to make more military personnel available for combat or other positions that only they can hold.

planning efforts will explicitly consider areas critical to the successful execution of the corporate strategic plan.[4]

The framework in Figure 3.1 depicts relationships among strategic intent, guidance, and plans from a corporate perspective as well as from the functional and business unit perspectives described next.

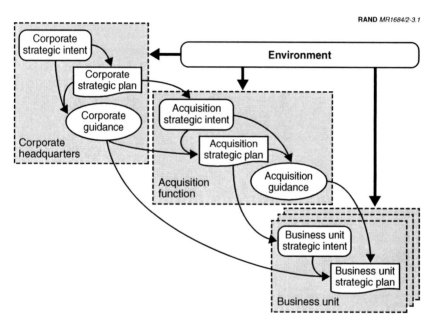

Figure 3.1—Relationships Among Strategic Intent, Guidance, and Plans from Multiple Organizational Perspectives

---

[4]Of course, it is difficult to know a priori what aspects of corporate strategic intent will affect human capital strategic planning in various parts of the organization. The task of corporate planners is to tailor the guidance to the needs of the organizations doing the planning. For example, it is unlikely that all aspects of the DoD's strategic intent will have a major impact on how the acquisition community carries out its business. In this case, the corporate guidance would identify and clarify particular themes or directions the department intends to take and which require actions on the part of the acquisition community to accomplish. Some—perhaps many but probably not all— would have human capital implications.

The Functional Perspective

As we have described, the corporate strategic plan sets the context for functional strategic intent. It defines, or at least informs, the functional purpose, mission, and vision. To lend specificity to the discussion here, we use the acquisition function as a representation of one of the many functions in an organization.

Functional planning emphasizes two distinct interests.[5] From an *operational* perspective, planning focuses on the overall conduct of functional activities, that is, How will the overall organization and each of the components carry out the major responsibilities of the function? From a *resource* perspective, planning focuses on the management of the members of the workforce who make up the functional community.

Corporate guidance, implicit or explicit, defines major areas of emphasis that a function should address in its strategic plan. To convey its strategic intent and to translate that strategic intent into concrete actions, the function can rely on published documents or on ad hoc policy statements. In DoD, for example, the acquisition function's strategic intent can be found in such documents as a military department mission statement, strategic plan, and ad hoc policy statements. Other functional areas (financial management, legal counsel, information management, etc.) may provide strategic intent in the form of guidance as well.[6]

As with corporate planning sources, these documents reflect the functional leaders' judgment, in this case, as to how the function can best contribute to accomplishing the overall corporate strategy. Similarly, the human capital implications of this intent are often not

---

[5]As an organizational entity, this function may reside at several levels within the organization (in the DoD, for example, the acquisition function exists within the OSD, military department headquarters, major commands, and even at business units). For the purposes of this report, however, we discuss the function as a single entity.

[6]For the purpose of human capital strategic planning in general and workforce planning in particular, guidance from the human resource management function is especially important. It primarily shapes, however, the design of human resource management policies and practices (for example, guidance regarding diversity and prevention of sexual harassment), rather than the way the business unit carries out its business.

clear. By articulating clear functional guidance[7]—either in these documents or separately—functional executives (at all organizational levels) can directly influence how the function will be carried out (and, thereby, contribute to accomplishing the overall corporate strategic plan).[8]

The Business Unit Perspective

Finally, a functional strategic plan can set the context for the strategic intent of the business units, and the corporate and functional guidance can define major areas of emphasis for each business unit to address in its strategic plan. Business units should—and do—choose to carry out their activities according to different strategies (for example, to deal with different industries, customers, and products). Clear guidance from the corporate headquarters and the function is especially important to ensure that the strategies of all the business units (though necessarily heterogeneous) are aligned with the direction the senior corporate and functional leaders choose.

The business units contribute directly to carrying out the mission of the overall organization. The business units are the point of the spear. The corporate headquarters and functions exist to enable and support the business units. In addition, in terms of human resource decisions, business units are in the best position to understand their human capital needs, and their actions will have the major impact on meeting those needs. Business units most directly influence the people in the workforce: how they are hired, organized, assigned, developed, rewarded, and separated; how their performance is measured and managed and their succession planned; who remains and who leaves. Managers can implement policies and practices affecting these activities in a way that purposefully seeks to effectively execute the overall strategy of the organization and the strategy of the functions—or in a way that simply takes the path of least resistance, rely-

---

[7]As with the term "corporate guidance," *functional guidance* (as we employ the term in this report) is the vehicle for identifying and transmitting those aspects of functional strategic intent that directly affect human capital strategic planning.

[8]For example, in preparation for the first application of workforce planning in the defense acquisition community, the OSD included guidance to "shift from managing supplies to managing suppliers," to emphasize a change in the way the acquisition function would be performed in the future.

ing on local decisions that maintain the status quo. Many organizations may follow the second path, not through managerial ineptitude, but because guidance and planning processes are not available to clearly mark the preferred path.

Both the guidance and the planning processes are important; neither one by itself will result in business units aligned with the strategy of the overall organization. Many business units have a strategic and/or business plan. How well these plans reflect the direction the corporate headquarters and the functions want to take varies, in part because that direction must often be interpreted by the business units. Clear guidance is essential if the leaders of business units are to fully align their activities with the overall organization's strategy. This is particularly true if the overall strategy is changing. But even with clear guidance, the business units must be able to translate the implications of that guidance into decisions that affect people, their culture, their organization, their characteristics, and their behaviors. This requires a set of processes. Workforce planning is one such process. Employing the workforce planning process solely within the context of the business unit, however, is not sufficient. The strategic intent and strategic plans of the corporate headquarters and the functions must drive that process.

Additional Observations

As Figure 3.1 suggests, the environment is a pervasive factor in overall strategic planning. It influences all organizational perspectives. It is the source of external pressures. These pressures affect each perspective differently. The corporate and functional guidance are vehicles for communicating the higher-level environmental impact to the business units.[9]

The limit of the preceding discussion is that it focuses on only one aspect of strategic planning: conveying strategic intent. Other as-

---

[9]For example, in preparation for the first application of workforce planning in the defense acquisition community, the OSD included guidance to "fully implement the intent of DAWIA [the Defense Acquisition Workforce Improvement Act] to maximize the consideration of and compete civilian and military personnel for acquisition positions to select the 'best qualified.'" This statement reflected external pressure, in this case congressional pressure.

pects of strategic planning are needed to convert this intent into desired results, to develop measures of how well the organization is achieving those results, and to review desired and achieved results periodically. Although this feedback is omitted from Figure 3.1, it can be critical to successful strategic planning.

HUMAN CAPITAL STRATEGIC PLANNING: LINKING HUMAN RESOURCE MANAGEMENT POLICIES AND PRACTICES TO STRATEGIC INTENT

In our framework, *organizational* strategic planning revolves around the leaders' expression of corporate, functional, and business unit strategic intent. Human capital strategic planning is one component of organizational strategic planning. It focuses on identifying and implementing an aligned set of human capital policies, practices, programs, processes, and systems needed to accomplish the organization's strategic intent. An organization can carry out human capital strategic planning from the corporate, functional, or business unit perspectives. This report focuses on the business unit perspective.[10] In our framework, human capital strategic planning begins with an assessment of the environment, consideration of corporate and functional guidance,[11] and clear articulation of the business unit's own strategic intent as it relates to decisions regarding its human capital.

At least four separate processes reflect the scope of comprehensive human capital strategic planning: cultural shaping, organizational design, workforce planning, and performance planning. Cultural shaping focuses on organizational values. Organizational design focuses on the overall structure of the organization, the locus of authority within the organization, and the relationships among the various parts of the organization. Workforce planning focuses on

---

[10]Human capital strategic planning, as we characterize it here, may be effectively conducted above the business unit level, particularly if the business units are relatively homogeneous and if business unit leaders actively participate in the planning activity.

[11]Corporate and functional guidance transmits the aspects of corporate and functional *strategic intent* that influence human capital strategic planning at the business unit level. We generally employ the term "organization's strategic intent" to mean "corporate and functional guidance and business unit strategic intent."

workforce characteristics—measures of the latent human capability within an organization. Performance planning focuses on behaviors—the means of putting that latent human capability into action.

Taken as a whole, the objective of these processes is to develop polices and practices that align values, structure, characteristics, and behaviors with the strategic intent of the organization.[12] Of course, these individual processes and the policies and practices they evoke are interrelated. So, although the organization ideally carries out the processes simultaneously, complexity may argue against such an approach. The most prudent course for an organization may be to consider them separately, keeping in mind the end goal of aligning policies and practices in a comprehensive and integrated human capital strategic plan.

In addition, the planning process identifies systems (for example, a human resource management information system, a Web-based employee portal, a skill assessment system) and human resource management processes (for example, the recruiting and hiring process, the succession planning process, the outplacement process) needed to support human resource management throughout the organization. In our experience, particularly in the federal government, these systems and human resource management processes are often the primary focus of a headquarters' deliberations regarding human resource management, strategic or otherwise. For example, the headquarters may leverage technology (say, in the form of a Web-based or Web-enabled portal) or may reengineer a process (say, removing time-consuming obstacles from the hiring process) to reduce costs. These activities solve the more concrete and visible problems, but they may not significantly enhance organizational performance, particularly in the rapidly changing environment of a business unit.

---

[12]This highlights an important point: Even when human capital strategic planning is conducted by the business unit, the goal of the planning is a set of human capital decisions that support the organization's strategic intent—not solely the business unit's strategic intent. The corporate and functional components of the organization's strategic intent are brought to the business unit analysis through corporate and functional guidance. Thus, the degree to which the human capital strategic plan supports the organization's strategic intent is directly influenced by the clarity of the corporate and functional guidance provided.

Therefore, we recommend a human capital strategic planning framework that places system and human resource management process considerations in the background. Are these systems and processes useful? Yes. Necessary? Yes. Primary? No. Our human capital strategic planning framework envisages an implemented set of human resource management policies and practices aligned with the organization's strategic intent and with each other as a principal means of profoundly influencing organizational performance. The systems and human resource management processes enable and support that end.

The actions required to implement an aligned set of human capital decisions are captured in a human capital strategic plan, generally unique to a particular business unit. But a plan is only as good as its effect on organizational performance measured in terms of the outcomes it seeks to accomplish. This feedback completes the picture of the human capital strategic planning activity. Figure 3.2 portrays this complete framework from the business unit's perspective.

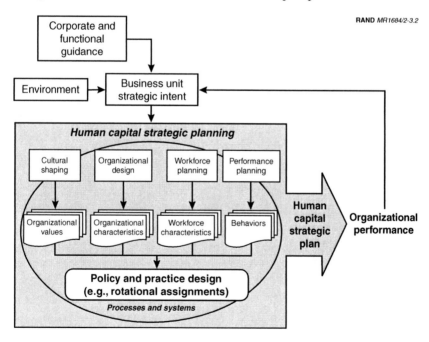

RAND *MR1684/2-3.2*

Figure 3.2—A Framework for Human Capital Strategic Planning

Four Questions

Workforce planning, in our framework, is intended to ensure that the organization's investment in human capital results in the timely capability to effectively carry out the organization's strategic intent. To reach this goal, workforce planning addresses four fundamental questions about the characteristics of an organization's workforce:

1. What critical workforce characteristics will the organization need in the future to accomplish its strategic intent, and what is the desired distribution of those characteristics?

2. What is the distribution—in today's workforce—of the workforce characteristics needed for the future?

3. If the organization maintains current policies and programs, what distribution of characteristics will the future workforce possess?

4. What changes to human resource management policies and practices, resource decisions, and other actions will eliminate or alleviate gaps (overages or shortages) between the future desired distribution and the projected future inventory?

From a casual consideration of these questions, one might conclude that this is an activity the organization can delegate to the human resource management department. And in many organizations that do workforce planning, that is where the activity is located—and localized. However, we believe that workforce planning, viewed as a tool to change how an organization does business, requires a broad base of active participation (by different functions and different levels), a shared understanding of and commitment to the goals of the workforce planning activity, and a purposeful assessment and clear description of where the leaders want to take the organization. In our view, human resource management departments—no matter how strategic—cannot effectively conduct workforce planning without executive sponsorship and active participation. Effective workforce planning, then, requires extensive leader direction, support, and input. In Chapter Four, we outline the roles that executives must play.

EXECUTIVE ROLES IN WORKFORCE PLANNING

Three major executive responsibilities underpin workforce planning:

- formulating the organization's strategic intent as the basis of workforce planning
- organizing for workforce planning (establishing the organizational roles and relationships, ensuring communications, etc.)
- eliciting the contribution of the appropriate participants to carry out workforce planning.[1]

How do these responsibilities play out?

PARTICIPANTS AND ROLES

Because of the strategic nature of workforce planning and the reliance on data, individuals responsible for corporate planning, technology, information systems, and operations provide necessary input. However, four other groups play a critical role in actually conducting effective workforce planning: senior corporate executives, business unit executives and line managers, functional community managers, and human resource managers.

---

[1]This is not a novel characterization. Rather, ignoring wording changes and revised orientation, these are the functions of the executive delineated by Barnard in 1938 (Barnard, 1968).

Senior Corporate Executives

All parts of a large and diverse organization exist to accomplish a common end. The senior corporate executives of the organization establish the strategic direction: what the organization will do and how the organization will carry out its mission. The most important contribution they can make to the workforce planning activity—and to accomplishing overall organizational goals—is clearly articulating a comprehensive statement of corporate and functional guidance that business unit leaders can relate to human capital needs in the future. Senior corporate executives can use corporate and functional guidance as a direct means to extend their strategic reach into the organization they oversee.

Senior corporate executives also play a key role in setting the context for successful workforce planning by establishing the structure for and sustaining active lines of communications throughout the organization. Vertically, they determine and assign the appropriate roles to the different levels of the hierarchy (that is, what they want the participants to contribute to the workforce planning activity); horizontally, they eliminate the communication barriers between the line organizations and the functional staffs, and among the functional staffs. Senior corporate executives sit at the top of each of these stovepipes, and a well-articulated and shared perspective regarding the need for and value of workforce planning is the foundation upon which effective workforce planning is built.

Senior corporate executives can champion the activity, expending their time in ways that communicate to their peers and subordinates the importance of the workforce planning activities (and eliciting their active participation in it). However, they must also act on the results of workforce planning. They are in the position to acquire needed authorities and resources. In some cases this may mean taking on hard challenges, but without this commitment, their efforts and those of many others carrying out the workforce planning activity may be wasted.

Thus, the workforce planning activity not only begins with senior corporate executives setting direction, it also returns to them for action.

Business Unit Executives and Line Managers

A business unit's leaders—in particular, its executives and line managers—develop the strategic intent of their organization in the context of their environment and the guidance they receive from above. They are in the best position—and are charged with the responsibility—to determine what activities to engage in and how to carry out those activities. Likewise, they are in the best position to identify the characteristics of the workforce needed to carry out those activities most effectively. The workforce planning activity gives them the opportunity to frame those decisions explicitly in the larger strategic context they bring to the planning table.

To support effective workforce planning, business unit executives and line managers may need to restructure their organization. This might entail formally integrating workforce planning into the existing organizational strategic-planning framework. In addition, business unit executives and line managers must position workforce planning as a business unit activity—not something delegated to the human resource management department.

Business unit executives and line managers communicate the activity as an important "executive time-out" through their active participation in the activity and by selecting other participants who are innovative in identifying how people contribute—and how they can contribute—to business unit success. Business unit executives and line managers can make participation in the workforce planning activity a key developmental experience for prospective business unit leaders. Business unit executives and line managers do the most to establish the importance and value of participation in workforce planning by acting visibly on the results of workforce planning. In particular, they enhance its importance when they rely on the business case developed through workforce planning to make decisions on requests for authority and resources and to explain potential changes in policies and practices to the workforce.

Functional Community Managers

Many organizations assign career development and other human resource–related responsibilities for individuals in specific occupational or professional groups to senior executives in the occupation or professional group. In addition, senior functional executives often oversee these types of responsibilities for individuals working in major functional areas (such as acquisition or finance).[2] We are concerned here with the functional community managers (although most of what we say is applicable to managers of occupational and professional communities as well). These functional community managers have an important executive role in defining a vision for the community and developing a career management strategy for achieving that vision. The vision can be a means for ensuring that the capabilities provided by the function are tailored to the potentially changing needs of the organizations that use the function.

In effect, functional community managers serve a dual role: balancing the needs of the organization with the health of the community. Functional communities usually span the entire organization; they are seldom localized at a particular business unit. Therefore, functional community managers carry out their role through a structure that exists at multiple levels in a large organization. The higher levels provide a horizontal view of the function across the organization, focusing on the viability of the overall community; the lower levels provide the link to business unit needs and counseling to individuals. Effective executive communication among these levels is particularly important in view of the potentially conflicting nature of the dual roles.

Because a function exists primarily to serve the needs of the business unit, functional community managers have an important role in identifying how the function can contribute to the success of the business unit in the future. Thus, they can provide another executive voice to motivate participation in the workforce planning activity by business unit executives and line managers. Their focus should be on soliciting information to help them determine how they can help the business unit executives and line managers improve organizational performance.

---

[2]Within the defense acquisition function, this functional community management arrangement is especially prevalent, including Directors of Acquisition Career Management formally established within each military department in accordance with DAWIA requirements (Title 5, United States Code, section 1705).

Human Resource Managers

Currently, the most difficult leadership challenge to human resource managers in supporting workforce planning may be in organizing the human resource management function to respond to the needs of the line and community managers. Human resource managers will need to engender creativity and motivate their human resource management professionals to identify, develop, and apply innovative human resource management policies and practices that effectively close the gap between the characteristics the organization will need and those the workforce is likely to possess. They need to formulate and carry out an organization-centric vision and strategy in order to bring this about. Doing so will undoubtedly require a shift in the requisite competencies of human resource professionals, potentially setting in motion a workforce planning effort focused on the human resource management community.

Although human resource managers should not conduct workforce planning as a compartmentalized internal function, they generally are the most natural proponents of workforce planning in an organization. Some part of the organization needs to facilitate the activity, understand the state of the art, maintain the information systems, and develop workload and inventory projection models; human resource managers are the natural focus for these activities. This is a different role than many human resource managers play today, and doing human resource management business differently may require restructuring. Human resource managers also need to form strong partnerships with the community managers because they share many of the same objectives (maintaining the health of the workforce) and designing the tools for accomplishing those objectives are the purview of the human resource manager.[3]

---

[3]Although the military departments have managed the career development of the military workforce by communities (such as the infantry branch, or aviators, or surface warfare officers) managing the career development of the civilian workforce by community (or function) is a relatively new approach. The focus on managing civilian communities initially gained visibility, in large part, from a congressional mandate to manage the acquisition workforce. Both the military and civilian community management approaches are highly centralized. The military human resource management function manages the military workforce by community. However, within major functional areas, civilian functional staff (not civilian human resource management staff) most often manage career development of the civilian workforce within that

In the role of workforce planning proponent, the human resource manager also has responsibility for ensuring the integrity of the activity. This means soliciting active participation of business unit executives and line managers and community managers. The human resource manager plays a key role in meeting the second purpose of workforce planning: developing an aligned set of human resource management policies and practices that will ensure the appropriate workforce will be available when needed. This endeavor, as much as any other, will motivate active participation in workforce planning. Table 4.1 summarizes the executive roles of the senior leaders participating in the workforce planning activity.[4]

---

function (or community); the partnership with the human resource management function (at least as we have observed it) is not particularly strong. We found, however, a particularly good example of a strong partnership between the community managers and the human resource managers—and line managers—at the Naval Facilities Engineering Command (NAVFAC).

[4]As in the discussions above, this summary is intended to apply to senior corporate leaders at the headquarters levels and to functional community managers and human resource managers at all levels.

Table 4.1

Executive Roles in Workforce Planning

	Formulate Strategic Intent	Organize for Workforce Planning	Interest and Motivate Workforce Planning Participants
Senior corporate executives	Formulate corporate and functional guidance with implications for human capital	Assign appropriate workforce planning roles to different perspectives and levels of the hierarchy	Generate the need; identify the benefit; act on results; take on difficult changes
Business unit executives and line managers	Articulate business unit strategic intent in terms of its human capital implications	Integrate workforce planning into organizational strategic planning	Actively participate; act on the results
Functional community managers	Specify a vision and a community-management strategy for the functional community	Align community management structure to respond to business needs	Promote partnership between line managers and community managers
Human resource managers	Formulate an organization-centric human resource management strategy	Sponsor workforce planning; develop center of excellence	Develop innovative human capital solutions to problems identified during workforce planning

Chapter Five

RECOMMENDATIONS

We summarize the major points of this report in the form of actions that leaders should take to ensure effective strategic workforce planning. We also offer some concluding observations regarding when leaders should actively participate in workforce planning.

ACTIONS LEADERS SHOULD TAKE

These recommendations apply to corporate executives, business unit executives and line managers, community managers, and human resource managers.

Institute Workforce Planning as Part of Organizational Strategic Planning

As the sponsors and primary beneficiaries of strategic planning for the organization, leaders can tailor planning activities to meet their needs. If an organization is fundamentally changing how it wants to do business, workforce planning (and other human capital strategic planning processes) can become a powerful means of moving toward the desired goal. Leaders should ensure that workforce planning becomes a key component of their strategic planning activities with the expressed goal of aligning human capital capabilities with their long-term goals.

Provide Clear Guidance

To use workforce planning—and strategic planning, generally—as part of the means to align the efforts of the organization with overall strategy, clear guidance is essential. Leaders must provide corporate, functional, and business unit guidance in concrete terms that are meaningful to those in the organization charged with carrying it out. Often, strategic plans (and more-general statements of strategic intent) are composed of lofty phrases. Such presentations can be valuable for motivating action, but they are usually not useful for execution. In the case of workforce planning, leaders need to provide clear guidance—guidance that translates corporate, functional, and business unit strategic intent into terms that have implications for the workforce capabilities needed to carry it out.

Ensure the Right Participants

It is probably in the fundamental nature of organizations that the right participants to engage in workforce planning have other, equally important responsibilities competing for their time and attention. If strategic planning (including workforce planning) is to be successful, leaders must understand it as an appropriate "executive time-out." Leaders must resist the urge to delegate the workforce planning activity to the human resource management department and retain only final review authority. Workforce planning benefits from the diverse views of participants from different levels and different functions. Leaders must motivate themselves and others to explicate those perspectives as an integral part of the activity.

Lead the Effort—Physically and Intellectually

It is one thing to direct an effort, another to participate fully in carrying it out. Although functional experts and analysts can most efficiently and effectively conduct much of the workforce planning effort, leaders are best suited—indeed, uniquely suited—for key tasks. The most obvious are those related to articulating and communicating strategic intent; however, business unit line managers play a key role in developing the policies and practices, as well. Leaders often signal the importance of an activity merely through their willingness to "be there." They significantly enhance that signal by leading the effort intellectually.

Focus on the Business Case

A business case is seldom formulated in the human resource management arena. People are innovative; they have little difficulty generating "good ideas" that are unsubstantiated by the insight and rigorous analysis that produce a business case. Faced with such "good ideas," leaders must ask whether the potential return on the investment is worth their cost. A business case explicitly lays out the rationale between an organization's strategic intent and the human resource management policies and practices it needs to accomplish that intent. A business case identifies the impact of the leaders' strategic intent on how the organization does business and how it affects the workforce. It highlights the gap(s) between the workforce needed to accomplish the leaders' intent and the workforce the organization expects to have assuming continuation of its current human resource management policies and practices. A primary purpose of workforce planning is to develop a business case for securing authority for new or modified policies and practices and for allocating resources to human resource management programs. Leaders should demand business cases that are as solid as those for investments in technology, equipment, or facilities.

Monitor Results

What is measured, matters. Workforce planning is not a one-time activity—especially in a rapidly changing, uncertain world. The organization needs to conduct the activity as frequently as it is likely new information would change fundamental decisions. If integrated into the overall strategic-planning process as suggested above, workforce planning should be conducted during the same cycle. As leaders monitor the results, they demonstrate yet again the importance of the workforce planning activity. In addition, leaders can assess results over time and adjust the activity accordingly.

Act

Actions speak louder than words. When workforce planning produces a viable business case, leaders must act on it. Without follow-up, the workforce planning activity will atrophy. The leaders' actions may not always succeed; but the effort that goes into building the business case is wasted if leaders ignore the business case.

CONCLUDING OBSERVATIONS

The value of active executive participation in workforce planning is proportional to the magnitude of change they intend in the organization and the importance of human capital in bringing about that change. If the environment, product mix, and customer base are relatively stable and if well-understood organizational processes are expected to continue, tactical workforce planning provides an effective means of managing normal turnover. In such a case, the value added by executives' participation (of the sort outlined in this report) would almost certainly not be worth the cost in terms of their diversion from other executive activities. Workforce planning in this venue is an activity appropriately carried out by staff (community and human resource managers), with little involvement of senior leaders.

However, executives in an organization undergoing substantial changes in the nature of its business/mission or in how they seek to carry out that business/mission will find workforce planning an effective tool with which to translate their unique insight, perspective, knowledge, and understanding into concrete decisions. These decisions ensure that the appropriate workforce will be available when needed to implement the direction the executives chose. In such a situation, executives play key roles and contribute critical information to shape the application of workforce planning. Most important, active executive participation invigorates momentum for organizational change. Consequently, strategic workforce planning, integrated into the organization's overall strategic planning, promises very high dividends.

A companion report, *An Operational Process for Workforce Planning*, MR-1684/1-OSD, describes a methodology any organization can use to conduct workforce planning. This methodology was the basis for

the initial application of workforce planning in the DoD acquisition
community, completed during the summer of 2001.

Ballard, Tanya N., "GAO Puts Workforce Issues on 'High-Risk' List," *Government Executive*, http://www.govexec.com/dailyfed/0101/011801t1.htm, January 18, 2001.

Barnard, Chester I., *The Functions of the Executive* (Thirtieth Anniversary Edition), Cambridge, Mass.: Harvard University Press, 1968.

Bolles, Richard N., *What Color is Your Parachute?* Berkeley, Calif.: Ten Speed Press, 2002.

Department of Defense, *Rewarding, Organizing and Managing People in the 21st Century: Time for a Strategic Approach— Working Papers*, Report of the 8th Quadrennial Review of Military Compensation, Washington, D.C., June 30, 1997.

Department of Defense, *Quadrennial Defense Review Report*, Washington, D.C., September 30, 2001.

Fitz-enz, Jac, *Human Value Management: The Value-Adding Human Resource Management Strategy for the 1990's*, San Francisco: Jossey-Bass, 1990.

Fitz-enz, Jac, *How to Measure Human Resource Management* (Second Edition), New York: McGraw-Hill, 1995.

Fitz-enz, Jac, *The ROI of Human Capital: Measuring the Economic Value of Employee Performance*, New York: AMACOM, 2000.

Hax, Arnoldo C., and Nicolas S. Majluf, *The Strategy Concept and Process: A Pragmatic Approach* (Second Edition), Upper Saddle River, N.J.: Prentice Hall, 1996.

Hall, Douglas T., *Careers in Organizations,* Pacific Palisades, Calif.: Goodyear Publishing Co., 1976.

Hall, Douglas T. and Associates, *The Career is Dead, Long Live the Career,* San Francisco: Jossey-Bass Publishers, 1996.

Office of the Secretary of Defense, *Shaping the Civilian Acquisition Workforce of the Future,* 2000, http://www.acq.osd.mil/dpap/Docs/report1000.pdf, accessed June 23, 2003.

Phillips, Jack J., Ron D. Stone, and Patricia Pullman Phillips, *The Human Resources Scorecard: Measuring the Return on Investment,* Boston: Butterworth/Heinemann, 2001.

Voinovich, George V., *Report to the President: The Crisis in Human Capital.* Subcommittee on Oversight of Governmental Management, Restructuring and the District of Columbia, Committee on Governmental Affairs, United States Senate. 106th Congress, Second Session, http://www.senate.gov/~voinovich/pressreleases/humancapital.pdf, December, 2000.

United States General Accounting Office, *High Risk Series: An Update,* GAO-01-263, Washington, D.C., http://www.gao.gov/pas/2001/d01263.pdf, January, 2001.

Zemke, Ron, Bob Filipczak, and Claire Raines, *Generations at Work: Managing the Clash of Veterans, Boomers, Xers, Nexters in Your Workplace,* New York: AMACOM, 1999.